# Olly Fant takes a bath

drawn and told by Nitka

First published in Great Britain 1977 by Egmont Publishing Limited
in association with Methuen Children's Books Limited


Translated from the Danish by Hugh Young

ISBN 0 416 05290 8

Printed in England by Chromoworks

EGMONT/METHUEN

Olly-Fant and his friends always enjoy having a bath. 'Rub, scrub, scrub, rub, tra-la-la-la-la-la!' they sing at the top of their voices. It always sounds specially nice when you sing in the bathroom.

Olly's aunt Ella-Fant has given him a bottle of shampoo. They must all try it. 'Mind you don't get soap in your eyes!'

Teeth need washing too!
Smile at the world and the
world will smile with you!

They have to look in the looking-glass
to part their hair . . .

but they can all help each other to brush their backs.
Now they're all ready . . .

Oh, don't you feel fine when you're clean!

It has been raining, and there is still a big puddle outside the front door. And here comes a car . . .

Swish! The car drives right through the puddle, and . . .

. . . it splashes mud all over them! Olly-Fant and his friends were so nice and clean, but now . . . ! Just look at them!

‘Come on,’ says Olly-Fant, ‘we can’t go into town like this. We must start all over again!’

They rub and they scrub, but they don't sing this time. It's fun getting ready to go out, but not TWICE running! And they shampoo their hair and brush their teeth and part their hair and brush their backs . . .

At last they cheer up again and can smile at themselves.

But they decide to stay at home and do a jigsaw puzzle until all the puddles are dry, so that they won't risk getting another mud bath when they go out.